GETTING OVER MYSELF
(AND OTHER PEOPLE)

written by Emma Hodgkinson
illustrated by Helen Walker

Getting Over Myself (and other people) is a collection of poetry about realising the thrill of life and trying to survive it. Divided into four chapters, the anthology works through the experience of four different hormonal responses: dopamine, oxytocin, cortisol and finally, serotonin.

CONTENTS

To embracing the chaos.

DOPAMINE

INSATIABLE

Tonight I come home
In my pocket: a packet of fags
Across each cigarette, a phone number's scrawled
And twenty men are left in waiting.
One by one,
I smoke them all.

Tiny triumphs curl around my mouth in the body of smoke
A delicious consumption (gentle devouring).

Tonight I come home
In my pocket: a packet of fags.
Across each cigarette, a phone
number's scrawled.

TRUTH OR DARE

Go on again and tell me I was nothing
Me, the one that's dripping down your throat
I'll let you eat cake and you'll pretend that you're not blushing
even though behind the jam, my honey lingers on your tongue

Go on, really, erase the past few months
Where you melted in my body and tattooed your skin on mine
When you begged for my tomorrows and you promised me a lie

Please, I love it. Dispose of me completely
Let my ghost striptease indefinitely,
Because my body's dead and buried but your memories?
Oh, honey. Those I'll never leave.

ALCHEMY

I broke up with my past and now I'm flirting with uncertainty
Cold showers smacked me out of what's been long decades of
dormancy
You think you want me now, but love,
There's so much fucking more to me
You'll realise you're starving
Because so far you've survived on normalcy
So you'll try to drink me down, gulping
Swallowing me thirstily
But you're left insatiable, famished
This famine's for eternity
You'll never get enough
You'll be chasing gold so tirelessly
Energised (and mesmerised)
By each surprise of alchemy

APEX PREDATOR

I think you think I'm soft
When you taste honey on my tongue
And you think I think I'm lost
Until my sugar fills your lungs
Because the sweetness on my skin
Is both my weapon and my bait
At first you're chasing, soon you're choking
On me
Yes, you're my prey and there's no escape.

REINCARNATION

The wind came today like a punch in the face
Thank fuck for that, needed a fall from graceful pretenses
Pretending and believing my own story
That without you I'm living in some tragic purgatory
Melting in the sun and forgetting my own glory
Thinking I'm stagnating when I'm really transitory
And each moment is finite and I'm onto the next
Minute hour chapter lifetime so far from what I expected
Yesterday last night even five minutes ago
I forgot my own language but now I've remembered how to say
no.

JANE'S SONNET

I am no bird and no net ensnares me
I am no leaf and no branch holds me down
I am no brick; cement cannot lodge me
I am no road, I belong to no town.

Finding the joy in living without capture
Remembering how to be on my own
Breathing   freedom in pain, rage and rapture
Discovering love   through loving alone.

So thirstily I gulp down oxygen
Quick - lick my lips and taste the thrill of life
To find that there's no poison as potent
As fading away. There's no sharper knife.

So to myself I promise: no suicide,
No disappearing. Live, and be alive.

THE FEAST

Honey I'm home and haven't you heard?
The table's ready, dinner is served.
I think of my lips, my tongue, my teeth.
They pucker – poised – longing to eat.
I've starved myself for far too long,
Acting as though I didn't belong
In my very own throne,
Right at the head
I was feeding somebody else instead
So raise a glass, pass the knife,
It's time for me to eat up life.

COMING INTO CONSCIOUSNESS

I want to live deliberately
Seaweed and cigarettes and long drinks and strong coffee and
music that fills my bones

For days now (years)
I've tiptoed the precipice of a life that barely feels that barely
feels like my own (though someone told me it was)

So now
I'll jump
(Deliberately?) Deliberately
Into myself
I'll swim and scream and swallow up the corners of all my
oceans
Exhaustively deliberate

OLD AGE OXYMORON

Yesterday it was Monday and I placed two

Twenty-pound notes

(Still glittering with snowflakes from Saturday night's black
market

blizzard)

Into the hands of my therapist

In a conference room full of suits and pens, I watched synonyms
of

words I understand dribble out of my mouth along with breath of

expensive coffee and breakfast pizza

Is this what being an adult is? I ask a stranger in a bar

Tongue blue chest high eyes locked

(Skin sags)

But I don't fear each year like they tell me I'm supposed to

My pulse throbs harder

My veins run thicker

My mind dances quicker

And I'm more alive than ever before

YOU ARE ON YOUR WAY

As the air around me clenches (stiffens hardens and entrenches)
I start to (stop.) impersonate cement
Then I remember teenage midnights
Chasing gasps, rejecting insight
Choosing following and leaving
Hurting dancing sometimes bleeding
But always daring to believe in something more
So this time I won't settle (fade?) I'm not some precious metal
I'm out here feeling seething making my own way.

INDEFINITE DECADENCE

I'll never be dull, let that never be said
Let's protest mediocrity from the plinth of your bed
Wake up my skin
Unsettle my bones
Slave to nothing (though maybe hormones)
We'll knock on the sky and wait for the sound
You'll be my king but I'll wear your crown
You've taken a bite; now take your seat;
Santé, darling. It's time to eat.

REMEMBERING

Biting my lip till it bleeds
Porcelain piercing
A pink cushion of flesh
Ribbons of red stream
Out and in and down
Just to taste.
No fear, restraint
Just taste.

Letting my tongue run the length of my teeth
Discovering every corner
Remembering
How delicious I am

SYBARITE

Step into my world and let's take ourselves on holiday you can make up my
new name and I'll call you Salvatore and we'll chase after excess –
In hedonistic opulence and forget about the rules and then laugh about the
consequence
And you'll call me arrogant
And I'll call you self-indulgent
Then we'll toast to our demise and take a bow for our performance
And I don't know you really, maybe not that much at all
And you don't know me either but you know you still want more
And so you'll climb into my mind and then I'll recline in yours
And then tread each other's veins till we're blazing in the core
Our footprints will echo for centuries in an incessant replay
And we'll sleep finally satisfied from the decadence of a Monday

MAKE BELIEVE

It's sumptuously August, in my mind.
Heat glitters my skin
And leaves them blind.
My friends' laughter trills (in musical notes)
At old boys with beer and miniature boats
And we own the world – or at least the park,
Making promises and breaking hearts.
And I hold his jokes inside my hands and
Dish them out to all my friends
And we swap secrets like they're ours
They're hungry, starving, to devour
Us but we keep them as our audience
They're gagging, begging, just one glimpse.

CALENDAR
ISSUES

He has an April sort of view of me.

Light and tender, nervous and slow

He sees delicate pastel blossom swaying slowly to the grass

freshly cut for the first time after a cold winter spent alone.

Remembered as confetti spread across the tracks for newborn

bunnies singing songs of procreation

But oh, love. How can you not see?

I'm seething with August. Sweat sticking long hair to hot necks

The dirt under my nails is dark and the soles of my feet are hard

and the days are long the nights are thick and August drips down

every crack and smothers suffocates haven't you noticed the

way we women wear warmth envied by forest fires breathing in

gasps. Sighs. Heavy in desire and I run my fingers through my

hair and scream and shriek and drink the air and I ride my own

body into the sky

LONDON

Heartbeats hot breath thinking of tequila kissing –
We're trying hard now.
You ask me things, my body answers
Our fingertips don't touch
I undress you in my mind and know full well you've done the
same, when I see my body glinting in your eye

Quick hands hiding slow feet
Humble conversations lacing all that we've achieved
And here we are: our own ornate trophies denoting years of
success,
Taking turns to bathe in each other's applause

And here we are, now.
We put down our trophies - and unleash our shame,
Past and future regrets intertwine in the sheets,

And here I am now, breathing stale whisky (warm caramel),
Tasting ashtray on my tongue,
Trophies wiped clean from my face.
Laughter lounges around on my lips,
And I leave with nothing but your fingerprint pressed on the
back of my mind,
Warm caramel.

COMPLEX FEMALE CHARACTER

I'm bored of your confusion as if I'm the centre of some
collusion where my sole intent and purpose is simply to make
you nervous

Well I have some news, ding ding, yippee, it turns out there's
several aspects to my dripping femininity

I'm saying please and demanding more you're on a pedestal then
on the floor I'm careful with me but not with you and yet I'll
give up everything I ever knew
I'm glitter in black but white cashmere you'll bathe in my
laughter and drown in my tears I'm lifetimes of commitment and
I can't hold down a job and my mind is still but my veins they
throb I'm dreams and academia I'm outside and interior and if
this doesn't answer your question then I'd suggest don't ask
again.

SCHADENFREUDE

Watching you writhe is my favourite new sport,
Flailing around like you do.
Delighted to find you are not what I thought,
I recline to the spectacle of you.

I used to think I wasn't capable
Of deriving pleasure from pain
But I learnt most things are breakable
The first time you called me insane.

And now I sit, cherry coke in hand,
As you make it so easy to smile
And I exhale
All our dreams and all we had planned
And I swallow
Down
My new (thanks to you)
Schadenfreude lifestyle.

REMEMBERING THE MANIFESTO

As the air around me clenches,
(Stiffens hardens and entrenches)
I start to (stop.) impersonate cement
But I remember teenage midnights,
Chasing gasps, rejecting insight
Choosing following and leaving
Hurting dancing sometimes bleeding
But always daring to believe something more
So this time I won't settle (fade?) I'm not just precious metal
I'm out here feeling seething making my own way.

YOUR HONEY NIGHTMARE

Allow me to introduce myself.
Close your eyes, breathe me in,
Taste me on your tongue.
I'm the honey dripping down your throat,
Now the nightmare in your lungs.
Part your lips; count to three:
Your sweetest demon, mon cheri.

TOMORROW

I'm not very good at standing still
I get too bored and crave the thrill of chasing after something
else
Need to feel more than I've already felt
Maybe someone new to just adore me
But when they do, I just start yawning
Perhaps a different industry
Or I could learn a language, how to count to three
And soon I'm hungry again for more
There's no medicine for me –
The terminally bored.

OXYTOCIN

WINGS OVER FEET

I'm trying to stay grounded but you picked me like a flower and my roots had got old anyway no they only dragged me down and now I'm fresh cut, thorns off roses, midnight jasmine, I'm a bouquet, I'm the centre of your attention and I reek of early May and I'm drunk off my perfume and you're more sober than you thought and I'm dying by the hour now but I know I'll live on in the eternity of your thoughts

LET'S GET LOST IN EACH OTHER, AGAIN

Tear down the walls
And throw away the ceiling
And you and I
Endlessly intertwine
Our minds weaving together till my thoughts are on your tongue,
Your heart is in my hand,
My fingers in your hair and
Your eyes on every inch
Tangled together till
Well,
Never

LONGING

I want to know every room, corridor, corner in your mind
And I'm not sure which door to knock on first
So instead, I'll stare,
In awe of your architecture,
Waiting for you
To invite me in

RUTH

I want you to revive me
Make me feel alive
Undeniably and unapologetically
Woman

Your eyeline draws a stencil of my shape
Dripping
Over my form
Reminding me of myself

Place your fingertips on my skin
(My cells are ignited,
neurons electric)
And I'm
undeniably

Unapologetically
Woman

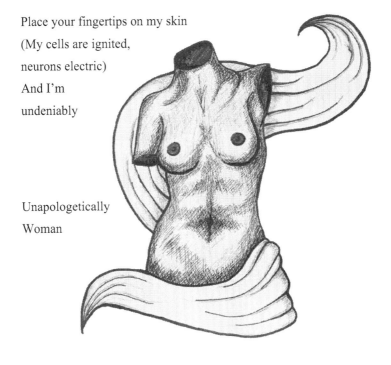

SHORT TERM BENEFITS, LONG TERM GAIN

We said hello on the Piccadilly Line
Pretending not to be strangers until act removed intention
Tremonti fingertips and a Sondheim smile
You spoke to my darkest corners and made them feel bright
We laughed, you held, I pushed, you held
Dancing in empty tubes eating picnics on the bed
You were fixed and I was broke so you caressed inside my head

We said goodbye on the Piccadilly Line
It ached more than I would've thought
But the clock got the better of us, time beat us out
So instead I'll leave you here
On the Piccadilly Line
Dancing in the empty tube carriages of my thoughts

I'M NERVOUS NOW

Holding words in my mouth like
Blueberry bubble-gum
Savouring sweetness
Melting on my tongue,
Knowing if I blow,
They'll pop
And you'll go.

YOUR RHYTHM

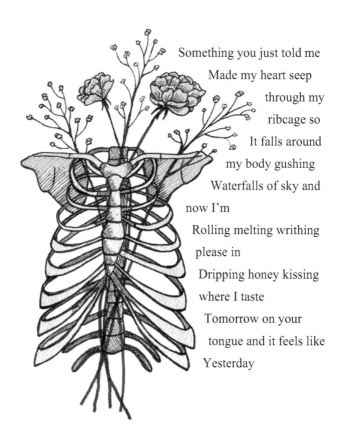

Something you just told me
Made my heart seep
through my
ribcage so
It falls around
my body gushing
Waterfalls of sky and
now I'm
Rolling melting writhing
please in
Dripping honey kissing
where I taste
Tomorrow on your
tongue and it feels like
Yesterday

ON THE TRAIN HOME

When I leave,
With me
You stay;
Your absence is full of you,
Teaching me to be alone.

Today on the train I found an invisible paper cup.
It's tied to a piece of string which laces down and round for
miles
and miles until it finds
You
(And your paper cup?)
And it hums with silent sound
Words that can't be heard but reach me nonetheless
And I (?) am completely alone.

DEUCES

Up swish smash and serve
The ball is in my court
You run around, leap up and down
But I'm accomplished at this sport

Up swish smash serve
　　You're getting out of breath
　　　　But don't lose hope, untie your rope
　　　　It's time to dance with death

　　　　Up swish smash serve
　　　　I look you in the eye
　　　　But you look back, lift up
　　　　your racket
　　　　And hit the ball up high

Up swish smash serve
Now it's me who's running round
You crack a smile and you smirk while
My face is in the ground

WALTZ IN A MINOR

You are milk and I am honey and we dine on each other all
morning long
You were always cool, and I was always funny
And we've never known right from wrong.
I wake you up and you show me my dreams
Though we never can get to sleep
We speak to each other through sighs and screams
Your eyes burn into mine till I weep.
I fortify my castle but you always invade
(Though you've got defences of your own)
I'm the Queen of Hearts and you're the Ace of Spades
Both willing, for now, to share the throne

WARRIOR

For the first time
In you
I've found a nation worth defending
So I will lead an army against myself
No chance of surrendering

An internal interrogation
Auseinandersetzung
It's open fire, the guns are out
(Ammo provided by Jung Ltd.)

I'm choosing to be a warrior
No masochistic victim
When losing you is the only defeat
And my torture, self-inflicted.

LONG DISTANCE

Hanging
On either side of the telephone line
Strangled by a language barrier

We stumble through linguistic mines
Divided by an unbridgeable gulf.
We shoot our words, but they don't seem to land,
Incomprehensible to each other's foreign ear.
And so we resort to nuclear communication,
Dropping bombs just to try to be heard

When all we had to do was remember the language we share:
When your skin whispers to my skin
And every cell understands.

CHARLOTTE

You and I are lemon trees.
We are long nights and hazy mornings
Cigarettes on rooftops

Slim Jim dancing giggling
At old men
Dying for us
Our skin smooth against their leather

And we run away, whisky breath
And cherry lips, working the
Upper Street runway with the
3am foxes and night-time rats
(We own the night)
We own the night.

You and I are lemon trees.
Cups of tea and tears
Hold my hand, let's stumble through solutions
Swapping retribution for eternal absolution
You and I are lemon trees.

MY ADONIS

Write me in your songs and I'll write you in my body I'm
hungover from your words, still I'm glittering, just groggy, and
you promised me ridiculous but rewarded me with more now
I'm writhing gasping melting I'm a puddle on the floor and you
think you're God or Jesus but you're far too dark for either – I'm
Aphrodite and Athena so we toast with honey tequila to the
people that we used to be, they barely feel like you or me

We swapped tentative for tenacious
we're sublime and we're salacious
and we're audibly audacious on the
hunt for the outrageous
And your plan? It came
together
And what's mine? I'm
chasing pleasure
So, honey,
Revel in my universe
And settle
Into the absurd

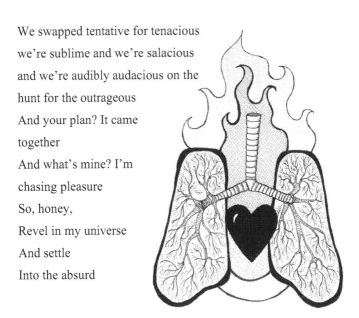

LEARNING

Place your fingers round my chest under
The creases of my wings.
Have me but don't hold me down too tight.
And if I choose to, I might fly
But I promise you one thing:
I'll always hang out just within your sight.

WRITTEN JUST BEFORE YOU FORGOT ME

It's days like these, when I'm most
Alive, I think about my effigy.
If I died – today – how would
you remember
Me? Am I immortalised in
stone,
Encased in cold rigidity,
Engraved onto your mind
In sculpted sublimity
Or is it the colours of my form:
Curves and lines and circles,
Pressed into paper perpetuity
Or maybe you'll forget
Me; words and pictures
lost.
Just a gap in your
memory, a space left
anonymously
Because we neglected to
ever emboss.

THIS TIME

I always thought love was about falling
And so I crashed and tumbled endlessly,
I confused fear for delight.
Chasing the pace and forgetting my grace,
Racing only to end with my face in the ground thinking
Perhaps I should reconsider.

So I thought,
Perhaps,
Love was climbing
And so I stretched, and I reached
- Forgot my feet
Focused only on my fingertips.
Sweat sliding as bones extended out of sockets,
Clawing the empty air above me.

But no,
Now,
I know.
Next you,
Any movement is undetectable.
But underneath, I sigh in relief,
At the rolling rhythm around my veins,
As I feel my heart start to grow.
Because next to you,
I know

AN INSTRUCTION MANUAL

With me, please take your skin off.
I want to tread your veins,
Navigate labyrinthine arteries,
Get lost along the way.

With me, please don't be gentle.
There's nothing that's too much.
You're the baby fawn but the hunter too,
I'm your weapon and your crutch.

With me, you don't need strength.
So please – finally – exhale.
Ease the aching muscles of your mind.
Find freedom in feeling frail.

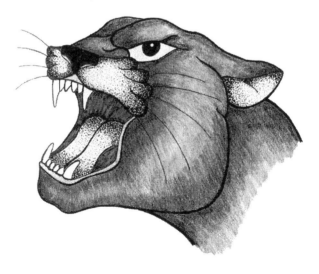

THE FUTILITY OF MISSING YOU

If I could be anywhere, I'd be in the middle of our very first
conversation
Instead I'm talking to the walls.
They staunchly listen to my festering drawl.
But I won't stop speaking as spit drips from my lips
A corpse in twitching rigor mortis
A drowned sailor bound to his beloved broken ship
I'll still miss you and remain remorseless.

RE-EDUCATING

I used to love like candyfloss, so
Sweet it sticks – I'm drifting off,
Diet coke clouds fizz constellations on my tongue.
Tastes like first dates (bound to go wrong)
Then it's neon colours through the night,
Something about - you only have one life?
Please, numb my head, and dim the lights,
This feels too much like dynamite.

So now
I love like old tree roots
Thick and gnarled and pushing through
The earth it holds me sturdily
So hurricanes pass harmlessly
No need for faking fervency
Communicating wordlessly
That thing about just living once
Is wrong. My next turn's just begun

CALIFORNIAN WINE

Well the heavens bloody opened and I'm here to taste the sky
and God I simply can't describe it but you finally gave me life
and I'm on a stage of fools but oh I'm taking the spotlight and
there may be violent ends but they came from our delights and it
looks like hell is empty because let's face it you are here and for
tonight babe you're all mine so let's toast,

To chaos,
And order,
And Californian wine.

CORTISOL

CABIN FEVER

Today I rode my bicycle through some streets felt like monopoly
Not money hotels houses just primary colours and monotony
My muscles sighed like puberty, heavy, too big for my body
Just these boulders sagging, dragging skin
They're punk teens playing hockey
And it's all discomfort now I'm dying,
Vying for attention
Can we pretend it's still affection, even though we both want
more

THANK GOD FOR RAIN

Thank god for rain. I needed that.
Drain my ever-climbing thermostat
I hadn't even noticed that
My skin was burning, blistered.

Thank god for rain. It's almost as though
All I've ever seen is snow
The ice froze closed every window
And numbed my fingertips.

Thank god for rain. Now I can forget
Every twat I've ever met
And most importantly (with no regret)
The me that I was yesterday.

QUARANTINED

I want to write a poem but I don't know how and this is unusual
for me. Last week I'd just tip my ear to the page and my
thoughts would come tumbling out.
But now I press my face to the ink there's no chance the two
might merge.
There's no bones inside my casket skull, no skeletons to purge.
Instead my head, replete with light, stings sharp with iridescence
Each corner suddenly exposed in blinding opalescence
And while the world speeds up, I lag. Quarantined behind a
window.
Imprisoned with the echo of an indefinite reflective limbo.

This woman I possess listens.

She laughs - and she gasps - and

She's amazed - and enthused –

    Trying desperately to disconnect from

      me.

      Black blood tickling her

      white skin.

      They can't see me (they

     don't look).

    They see her curves, her curls: their

     subordinate

Unaware I could swallow them.

Look like a flower; but be the serpent.

      This woman I possess

   impresses me.

Artificial   intelligence

Acting just as she should

Oh, she tries to ignore me,

If only she could.

Look like the flower; but be the serpent!

What?!

I'd rather not

But you give me no choice.

ARACHNOPHOBE

Swaying in the hammock of 5am I notice my eyes sink soft in
my skull.
My best friend's laugh and the intimacy of strangers spin and
loop around the room - like spiders' near invisible silk lacing the
air.
And we hang here – spiders or flies?
I thought I was the predator: the engineer of my environment,
curator of the night.
Strength which succeeds steel and a voice which tangles you up
in my designs.
And yet I wonder if anyone truly knows their role at any one
point before the moment they're swallowed whole.

MORBID CURIOSITY

If I look in with my gaze glued down so my eyes are under my
skin
Then I'm stuck with blood intestines and guts my troubles and
all my sins

And my sight gets stuck in this garbage truck of a brain
we're in
for a ride
Unable to
prise and
pluck
out my
eyes
In this
inevitable
mental demise

But if I look around not deafened by the sound of my thoughts
instigating a war
Then my eyes roam free and frolic friskily over subjects
unencountered before
And yet I'm so easily concerned with my own stupid words and
my feet and my head and my body
So I'll unglue my gaze from this self-imposed maze and try to
focus on what's actually around me

INSIDIOUS

Last week I looked at a man I hate, his face encased with lies – so easy to berate him – no surprise to find his words are dunked with prejudice, his violent speech explicitly igniting wars against another race so I screamed and shouted at my favourite enemy, my disdain pouring out so gracefully, can someone tell me how poison can be allowed to run a country?

And this week I spoke to a friend I love but quickly flinched as I caught sight of thoughts in her mind dribbling out iced in cyanide mixed with doubt of facts I thought indisputable but she thinks "well now discussion's on the table" we might ignore the abuse of minorities in order to put our faith in the authorities because "really it's in the benefit of you and me." And I recoil and wonder when the venom began to crawl its way through her veins.

Then tonight I sat back in my own head and browsed the library of my thoughts instead and visited everything I've ever said. I sat back pleased at all I'd ever achieved and awarded myself a philanthropic trophy and took some time to reflect – and entertain curiosities. But just one or two small footsteps in. I dropped. Straight. Flat. To my knees. In the dark corners of my body, toxicity tiptoed tentatively in a cloak of cocaine socialism and sung of ignorant optimism hiding in my privilege this venom's not new it's intimately vintage and it's infected every part of me contaminating systemically and I start to realise that poison has always run this country, and it didn't leave out me.

THE WEIGHT OF ABSENCE

This morning I lost the ring you gave me
And I cried for years

I cried for the loss
And I cried for the constant transience
For I have become all too familiar with impermanence

Something so solid and real it was wrapped around my finger,
Now: no longer there.
The space that's left behind carries the weight of all the things
I've lost along the way
Faces names words voices cities things I'd hoped for
Tangled into nonexistence and weighing down my hand

MISTRUST

Mistrust runs through my veins.
It always has.
Black blood
Gently rotting my body.
The softest destruction,
A festering fatality.

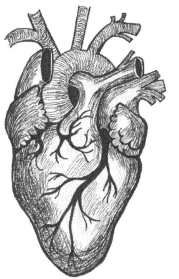

There's no emerald in envy,
Just glittering mould,
Running through my veins.
It always has.

The slowest destruction,
The most delicious disease –
Parasitical –
Feeding and chewing and gulping its way to my
Inevitable ending.

ODE TO MY FAVOURITE TOE

I've worked out what the problem is and it's that I'm always
hungry
Always wanting willing whining why my stomach won't stop
grumbling
Always looking to next year: a land where dream can all come
true
And yet I'm having trouble getting there
On this overcrowded commute
And then it comes to you: I pull and scrape and plead and beg
And you try so hard to please me but soon you're drained and
left for dead.
So I'm trying now to stop and maybe focus on my toes
These ugly stubs of flesh and nail and veins and blood and bones
They hold me so upright and balanced, clinging to the floor
And I recognise this gratefully and I never ask for more
So now I'm going to try to treat you like my favourite little toe
Because I'm truly grateful for you – more than you'll ever know.

THE VISITOR

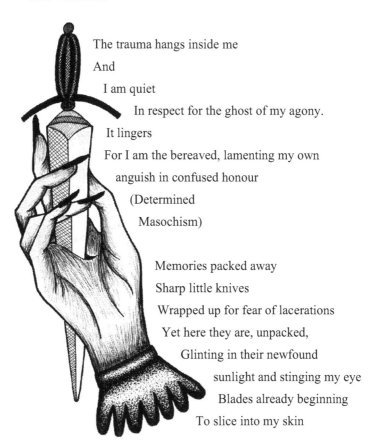

The trauma hangs inside me
And
  I am quiet
      In respect for the ghost of my agony.
    It lingers
  For I am the bereaved, lamenting my own
    anguish in confused honour
        (Determined
          Masochism)

              Memories packed away
              Sharp little knives
                Wrapped up for fear of lacerations
                Yet here they are, unpacked,
                  Glinting in their newfound
                      sunlight and stinging my eye
                      Blades already beginning
                    To slice into my skin

    The trauma hangs inside me

SERTRALINE

A large palm (of
Thick fingers,
Calloused skin,
Dressed in dirt and lines of years and years)
Is pressed to my face

Eyes hidden from the light.
I squeeze them shut
And hide my gaze from my captor
I hold my breath
Keeping my lungs to myself
As the finger pushes down on my tongue

Tears creep as my body aches for oxygen
Muscles weak and my bones beg for breath
Darkness shrouds as the palm presses harder
But I'm keeping my lungs to myself.
I'm keeping my lungs to myself.

HALLOWEEN

One day, a while ago, I made the mistake of slicing off the top of
my head.
And smiling, I sat
My brain spilling over my open skull
A bowl of treats ready and waiting for grubby fingered children
disguised as ghouls
And they push past each other to grab things fizzy and fantastic
And throw away the ones they don't like
And now, smiling, I sit.
The remnants of my mind left curdling
And I scrabble on the floor for the top of my head and place it
back and then I vow
Never
To take it off again.

I HAVE A TENDENCY TO LOSE THINGS

I lost my ring,
I lost one shoe,
I lost her laugh, and his words too,
I lost my mind, my dignity,
I lost a job, I lost a city,
I lost a friend, I lost my home,
I lost the ability to roam,
I lost my dream, some memories too,
I lost myself and I lost you.

In fact, I think I've lost a lot
So I'll try to stop now and take stock.
I seem to still have my fingers and toes,
My nails, my skin, my muscles and bones
So I guess I'll try to focus on that
And leave all that other shit in the past

IMPATIENCE

Metal cold against my skin the trigger's
Ready bullet's in glued to an endless
Precipice of waiting scorching no relief from
Heat I blister sweat rolls down my naked
Body aching now this pregnant silence
Smothers me as I lie down and
Count to three

IMPENETRABLE

Every diamond at one point was a piece of coal that did well
under pressure (her Instagram said to me)

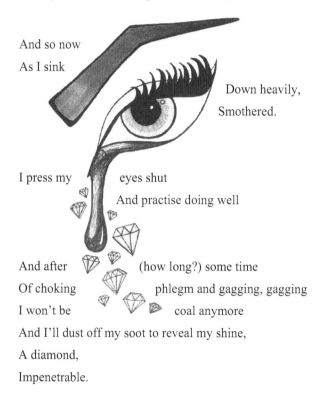

And so now
As I sink

Down heavily,
Smothered.

I press my   eyes shut
              And practise doing well

And after   (how long?) some time
Of choking   phlegm and gagging, gagging
I won't be   coal anymore
And I'll dust off my soot to reveal my shine,
A diamond,
Impenetrable.

PORTRAIT OF A LADY

The sitter's identity has unfortunately been lost,
Said the ink to the glazed over eyes.
Stylistic evidence suggests late 18th Century,
Likely when our artist won his prize!

The sitter's identity has unfortunately been lost,
Though it once sat in the Royal Academy!
Achieved (for our artist) instant acclaim,
For his valiant, vivacious virtuosity.

The sitter's identity has unfortunately been lost,
But can you see the glow of her face?!
A characteristic touch of white to enliven the eye,
How intimately the pigments
embrace!

The sitter's identity has
unfortunately been lost,
Though she lives on in eternal
memorial!
Untiring success for her
executioner
And a ceaselessly
anonymous pictorial.

INTERNAL/EXTERNAL

And now my body's stopped, my mind
Continues running round. Yes, it's racing darting
Chasing things - as I lay on the ground.
And my skin it groans and sinks into the floor
And tries to frown, but my brain ignores and
Beats its wings and sniggers at the sound

ME, ME, MONOTONY

I'm bored of being myself.
Or at the very least, this outer shell
It's a life I swear I didn't sign up for
I'd always thought there'd be something more than
Breathing sighing moaning crying waking up repeatedly trying
Victim to perpetual lying, social media's got me addicted to
buying
Till I'm left stone cold, my soul is drying
Propped up by self-indulgent writing
I'm just looking for something other than living or dying

So I wonder if I slipped out my skin,
Threw it away and jumped right in
To someone else's timetable:
A fairytale, a myth, a fable.
Maybe just someone far away
Not chained by handcuffs of the mundane
I'll hold constellations in my hands
Recline in oceans, dance in sands
I'll fall in love with something else
And transcend the boredom of myself.

FOR ELPHIN

The aggression of your absence has left my body bruised
Jab cross hook uppercut
Bleeding black and blue
I try to start my new life but it seems all I can do
Is hide under my bedcover from the ghost of you
I'm vomiting up old memories and choking on the new
You're in my books, my clothes, my shampoo
You're a fortress around me
Not sure I'll break through
Jab cross hook uppercut
Need to change my view.

TWENTY SOMETHING

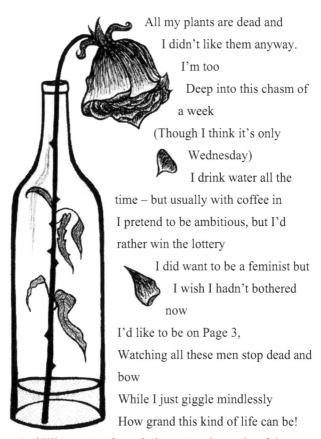

All my plants are dead and
I didn't like them anyway.
I'm too
Deep into this chasm of
a week
(Though I think it's only
Wednesday)
I drink water all the
time – but usually with coffee in
I pretend to be ambitious, but I'd
rather win the lottery
I did want to be a feminist but
I wish I hadn't bothered
now
I'd like to be on Page 3,
Watching all these men stop dead and
bow
While I just giggle mindlessly
How grand this kind of life can be!
And I'll two-step through the system in a colourful
monotony.

SPAG BOL SHAME

Do I miss being young? I miss
Spaghetti Bolognese
Today it's only served with this thick guilt glaze
Of sad cows ozone layers diameter of my thighs
And I can't stop them all, I have to choose my prize
And I pretend to be good and I want to be kind
But if I'm going to be honest about what's really on my mind
I'm simply far more concerned with the matters of my heart
Than every bloody one of my farmyard counterparts and how
The universe is dying and yes, I'm probably not trying
To do all the things I really should be.
And so I'll skip the carbohydrates and your minced flesh thanks
And I'll focus on getting into my new dress thanks
And you might call this vanity but I'm going to claim insanity
When all I want is
Spaghetti Bolognese
Yes thanks

REBIRTH

Your words were coarse, friction on my skin
And then (what's worse) I let you in
You scraped and pulled off every layer
While teaching me it was only fair
And for a while, I began to fade,
Growing smaller, I was weighed down
By the endless abrasion of your touch
Crumbling to ashes, it was all too much
But we underestimated frictional force
So I let the conflict run its course
And now prepare to be amazed
Because I'm on fire
And you'll burn in my blaze

UPSIDE DOWN REFLECTIONS

My head's at the foot of my bed and
My thoughts have moved to my toes instead
I painted the walls neutral (try and calm the mind)
But now I'm just blinded by beiges and browns so
Quiche what a cliché, it all comes around so I
Shouldn't bother anyway - might as well lie with my face in the
ground.
How tragic, such drama! I don't want to be calmer
Or getting any further than this literary murmur
You read but you can't hear me - don't look at me so
Sincerely!
I'm just here with my head at the foot of my bed instead.

A LOVE POEM

I love being loved. It's like fucking champagne.
Short skirts and cigarettes and methamphetamine
Kisses built from whisky breath
Make up smeared by rain
Relying on adrenaline
Numb to the pain

I love being loved. It feels like success.
A newfound posture with a puffed-out chest.
So you sit on your throne,
Because you beat the rest
But your seat's made of corpses
Of those you suppressed

I love being loved. It's what I always wanted.
How lucky are we to truly have bonded?
Though if I had the chance again,
I might not have responded
Maybe I took being on my own
A little for granted.

GET FIT QUICK

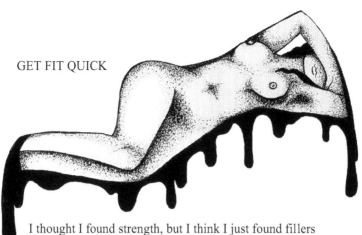

I thought I found strength, but I think I just found fillers
People and things and places
They filled up my skin and became my innards
And I walked around tall.

But the people walk off and the things end up broken and I
forget the names of the places
I start to deflate, a big bag of skin
No muscles to hold me upright

Old habits die hard and I'm soon searching for
A new face or home or title
Knowing they'll hold me up for a while
In this all too familiar cycle

WHAT YOU DESERVE

If their love
Doesn't fill every corner of your universe
Bubbling and frothing and dripping down your sides
Then it is not the love for you

For you are worthy
Of fireworks in your heart
That burn even oceans
And you are set alight

A DISAPPEARING ACT

There is nothing quite as deafening
As postcards left unread,
Spilling everything onto pages
That are left in a drawer instead.

It's like standing in a corner
And bawling at the wall.
Your screams whiplashed back in your ears,
Till you can't hear at all.

So you defend yourself with silence,
Knowing better than to speak,
Instead you give up trying
And morph into the meek.

And this is how it starts,
The gradual fading away.
You've been here before,
You just thought that this time,
You would maybe stay.

COPING MECHANISMS

Apparently I'm healing so I'm trying to feel my feelings but
they leave me
bloody reeling so I'm on the floor I'm kneeling is there some
other way of
dealing I tried hiding and concealing and just letting go
freewheeling but it sent
me through the ceiling so I'm trying to be more grounded but
this pain has got
me keeling over

It's not looking too appealing now but apparently I'm healing
now so I'll keep
trying to feel my feelings now.

BAD APPLES

Who would have thought that after all of that,
You would turn out to be nothing more than a bad taste left
sitting in my mouth,
Soon to fade completely
Leaving me only with enough memory to know not to bite into
bad apples again.

THE POWER OF HINDSIGHT

This year I lost an imaginary man.
Clumsy hands clutching at glowing colours
Surprised to learn that the rainbow
Was just a reflection refraction
Dispersion of my own ideas

This year I lost nothing
But an imaginary man.

MOVING ON

So here we go again,
Oops! Just like the last time when
My eye got lodged the wrong way round,
Stuck on the thoughts of yesterday,
Blind to sight and deaf to sound
Of anything ahead, I'm stuck behind.
I'm living in the last few months of my mind.

But I've done it before (and I'll do it again),
Heave my eyeball out its socket and then
Honour the pain, wallow a while;
Watch the blood congeal on the floor.
Wipe the face; gulp down the bile.
Now shove it back so it's facing the front
And look forward now. Go take what you want.

SERETONIN

ONWARDS

I lost my home
To a perfectly curated gallery of
Inanimate objects.
Designed to feel familiar

Suddenly strangers in my room.

Ribbons of time spent strangling
Each year so
Delicately
Fastened
Around
My
Neck

Who knew?!
That all I needed to do
Was just
To cut
Every ribbon
And use them to tie up the boxes of
my old life.

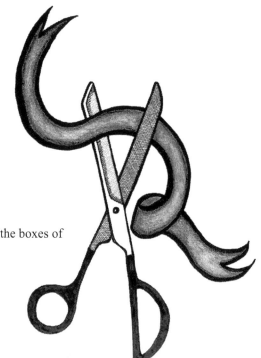

PLANS TO BEGIN IN MYSELF

Today I'm going to build a home inside myself
With soft floors to rest on
And windows looking out.
They will let the light in
And inside I will dazzle.

There won't be any corners
In my circular house.
There won't be any corners.

And once I've finished building,
I'll kick back and recline.
And there'll be no shadows in my circular house
And inside I will dazzle.

MORNING YOGA

Every so often
I clock out of my skull
And into my skin
Sink into each touch
How tantalising.

My own fingertips
Dance across my body,
The most intimate embrace
I've ever known.

Dripping honey
Lingers
On my tongue
The discovery of ecstasy in a
Tsunami of silk
Cascading over
Me.

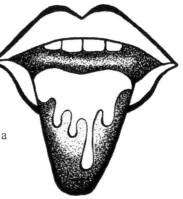

As each thought
Melts
My body grows heavy
And I soften into the earth
How tantalising.

DINNER FOR ONE (WITH KATE CHOPIN ON THE SIDE)

Taking a second

To remember my value, truly

Lying back in my own oceanic embrace

Knowing I am loved

Ceaselessly

And so I am seduced

By the murmurs of my own

heart

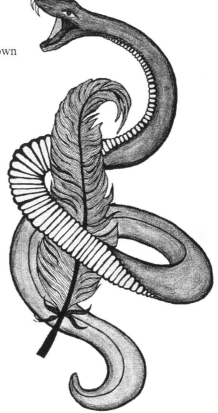

ON MY WAY

Give me a minute
For I have shed scales
Skin
A body
A year
A lifetime

So give me a minute
For now I roll like a new-born
Sensitive to sun

Yes give me one minute
While my tongue wraps round a language
And my own legs hold me high

So just give me a
minute
And find me
whole
Tall

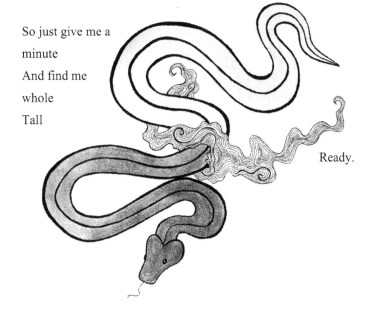

Ready.

DETACHING

Last quarter moon and I'm lounging in lilac
I'm giving up choosing and making my mind up
I'll bathe in perfume tainted with cigarette smoke
And dance on my tomb and stop laughing at bad jokes
And you'll blink as my decadence rolls out from each pore
Then again at my bruised knees as I roll on the floor
No impatience/agitation
I'm just here for today
And when the sun ends his scorching
I'll have melted away

EXHALATIONS

Like a concrete cloud
Dense. Heavy.
I will pour
Thunderous sighs
Drenching and flooding and heaving with everything inside me
My scream is a storm,
A final purging of the war in my mind,
The most magnificent ending to the most brutal of battles.
And my concrete cloud is gone
There's nothing but the river I left behind me
And I? Ha. I am the sky.
Stretching and expanding
In crystalline blue

SCAR TISSUE

Today I'm tracing my finger over old scars
and I don't find the pain of a wound
I once thought would weep forever. No
No. My skin stitched itself back together
and now sits thick. So you (the new
him? God.) will not
No. Not
be finding your way
in.

REMEMBERING HOW I FORGOT YOU

First, I think, I left your bed but
I left my jewellery there and then
Quite soon I left your flat but
I was still hanging in the air although
It wasn't long till you were gone from
My inbox, recent calls and I'm no longer
Knocking your front door or kissing in your entrance hall and
next
I'm off social media but we linger
In each other's brains – it's the end of a festival and starting to
rain
But shortly after you left that too and now all of a sudden
My body doesn't seem to remember you

COMING HOME

I found some space inside myself
(After realising there's been none for a while)
And now I stretch languorously
Taking a moment to recline in the feathered pillow of my brain
Arching my back and easing the tightness earnt through
centuries of
caged confinement

But don't worry.
I didn't clear you out
Just rolled and folded and tucked and gathered
    Arranged you onto shelves, into cupboards and drawers
        But there is a home for you here – in the corner of my
            mind
               Watching as I sprawl
               In all my own glory

END OF SEASON, NEXT

And as summer blisters into desiccated leaves
Azures wiped clean from the sky
I, too, leave all I had behind
Teetering on the precipice
Of my new life

And the crisp, cold air prickles my skin like sapphires
Smarting my eyes in jagged compression
But I smile, though shivering, in the knowledge
That through it all, I will glisten.

If I was a tree, I'd be a stump, I said to myself
today. I'm far from a mountain, I'm barely a
lump and it's unlikely that's going to change
I don't achieve much; my progress is slow;
I regret most things I say;
I can't do the splits, I can barely throw.
And let's not discuss the 5k.
I thought by this point, I'd tower high: my
branches tickling the clouds
And yet here I am looking up to the
sky from my puddle of pitiful doubt.
I imagine I'll soon disintegrate, if I keep moving
in this direction,
But when my mind collapses, my body
remains through some mockery of
divine intervention.
And if I dig my fingers in the soil, I
find something I forgot for a while:

My roots (cultivated through personal toil) lace the earth for
years and miles.
So though I'm still just a small stump now, turns out I'm rooted
in strength
So when it's time to stretch… stretch
I'll simply recline into new lengths.

LOOKING FOR SOMETHING IN ISOLATION

Blowing dust off books I'd meant to read
Hidden under old habitual speed,
Waking slowly with guiltless ease,
There must be something in isolation.

Teamed up against a faceless peril,
Suits suddenly drop all their quarrels
For chunky knits and pinks and florals,
Finding something in isolation.

And countries compete – not for war or sport
But ingenuity in their thoughts
Of how to offer the most support,
This is something in isolation.

The young are accepting possible fault
(Disproving archetypal revolt)
Doing what they can to save the old,
Finding each other in isolation.

GREEN FINGERS

And now it's clear to me that the garden of my tomorrow
I'd filled with trees and leaves and branches
Of you and us and nights and days and years
your voice my mouth our touch
Intertwining ivy leaves so green and rich and delicate

When in truth,
It all belongs to yesterday's soil.
And I laugh to myself,
As I look at tomorrow and see the barren patch of land,
Wondering how I ever thought I could be a gardener.

Then I look again to yesterday and find it bursting with life – so
dense and lush (your voice my mouth our touch)
And I smile because my past is beautiful.
So I look again to tomorrow and I see the empty soil:
Not barren, but glistening
In infinite arability

OVERDUE ARRIVAL

Take off the top of my head
And find
My body's overflowing
Bursting, brimming past capacity
My flowers won't stop growing
And so I'm blooming in all colours
Rose and teal and gold and purple
Scents so rich you're left intoxicated
I'm petrol, citrus, herbal
I've arrived in my own body after spending centuries
Naively chasing destinations
As though life was some striptease
Where you never reach the finish line
Because you're living in next year
But you'll never make it your today in this three legged race
with fear
So I cut the ties and realised
I have all that I need
It's all already inside me
My skin is laced with seeds
And perhaps you'll think I'm missing
Parts of life I'll never know
But I think you'll change your mind
So just sit back
And watch me grow.

END

Printed in Great Britain
by Amazon